My War
ROYAL AIR FORCE

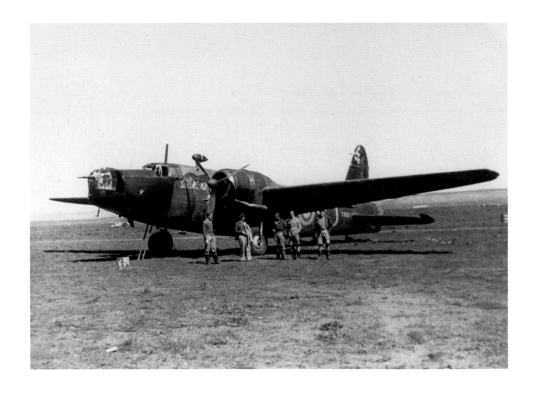

Peter Hepplewhite

Wayland

an imprint of Hodder Children's Books

Produced for Hodder Wayland by
Discovery Books Ltd
Unit 3, 37 Watling Street, Leintwardine, Shropshire SY7 0LW

First published in 2003 by Hodder Wayland, an imprint of Hodder Children's Books

British Library Cataloguing in Publication Data
Hepplewhite, Peter
Royal Air Force. - (My war)
1. Great Britain. Royal Air Force - History 2. World War,
1939-1945 - Aerial operations, British - Juvenile literature
I. Title
940.5'44941

ISBN 0 7502 4213 2

Printed and bound by G. Canale & C. S.p.A. - Borgaro T.se - Italy

Series editor: Gianna Williams
Designer: Ian Winton
Picture research: Rachel Tisdale

Hodder Children's Books would like to thank the following for the loan of their material:
Corbis: pp. 13 (top), 17; Hulton Archive: pp. 8, 9, 11, 13 (bottom), 20, 22 (top and bottom),
25, 27; Robert Opie Collection: p. 7.
Cover: both pictures from the personal collection of Ron Watts.

Discovery Books would like to thank the following for the kind loan of their material:
John Mills, Ron Watts, Harry Garthwaite, Thomas Douglas, Betty Williams, Ken MacMillan Studios and
the Shuttleworth Collection at Old Warden Park, Biggleswade.

Hodder Children's Books
A division of Hodder Headline Limited
338 Euston Road
London NW1 3BH

Contents

The Second World War Begins

In 1933 Adolf Hitler came to power in Germany and was soon threatening neighbouring countries. When Hitler attacked Poland in September 1939 Britain declared war. The war lasted six years and the Royal Air Force was in the thick of many battles. In this book, four RAF veterans and one member of the Women's Auxiliary Air Force share their wartime experiences.

RON WATTS

Ron was born in 1923 in Seaton Sluice, Northumberland. In 1942, he followed the example of his older brother and volunteered for aircrew. Trained as a fighter pilot, he became a flight instructor in Southern Rhodesia (now Zimbabwe) in 1944.

JOHN MILLS

John was born in 1920. He lived in Derby and was working as a Rolls Royce apprentice when he joined up in the summer of 1939. He trained as a navigator and fought in the Middle East and the Battle of the Atlantic.

HARRY GARTHWAITE

Harry was born in 1920 in Huddersfield. He was working as an insurance clerk when he joined the RAF in 1939. In 1940 he served as a night-fighter pilot before joining Met Flight (weather forecasting for Bomber Command) in 1941.

THOMAS DOUGLAS

Tom was born in 1925 in Rowlands Gill in County Durham. He came from a mining family and volunteered for the RAF in 1942 when he was still 16. Tom became a Sergeant Air Gunner in 1944 and flew photo-reconnaissance flights just before the end of the war.

BETTY WILLIAMS

Betty was born in 1923 in Everton in Liverpool. She worked as a typist for English Electric before she joined the Women's Auxiliary Air Force (WAAF) in 1942. From 1943 she served as a driver with 466 Squadron at RAF Leaconfield.

The RAF

When Britain went to war the Royal Air Force was quite small, with a total of 2,400 aircraft and 175,000 officers, both men and women. By May 1945, when the war in Europe ended, this had soared to 9,200 aircraft and over a million people. Of these 193,000 were aircrew – the people who flew the planes.

JOHN

It was only 23 years since the Battle of the Somme [in the First World War] and I didn't want to walk to war with a rifle. I joined the RAF volunteer reserve. I was too short-sighted to be a pilot so I trained as a navigator.

▼ Betty in her WAAF uniform sitting on a tractor.

BETTY

I was an only child and joined up to get away from home and my Mum. The uniform was very smart – it made you walk taller and feel proud of what you were. I made friends with some great people.

LET'S GO –

WINGS FOR VICTORY

◀ An RAF recruiting poster, 1939.

HARRY

I joined the RAF volunteer reserve on 9 May 1939. I knew conscription was coming and I didn't want to go into the army. I wanted to fly. We had lectures two nights a week on things like armaments and navigation. The idea of shooting down an enemy plane didn't seem as bad as having to shoot an enemy soldier – at least the crew had a chance to get out.

TOM

When I was 17 I was sent on a three-day selection course to see if I was good enough. All aircrew had to do this. You had to pass a medical examination and an intelligence test. My maths wasn't good enough for me to be a navigator so I said I would like to be an air gunner.

In six years of fighting over 70,000 RAF men and women died. Yet although losses were heavy there was never any shortage of willing recruits. The Royal Air Force was the most glamorous of the three armed services. Uniforms were smart and everyone who joined as aircrew became a sergeant or an officer on good pay.

Basic Training

Britain became a vast military camp during the war. The government took over land and buildings across the country to train millions of servicemen. Aircrew were sent to Lords Cricket Ground in London to be given their kit and an introduction to RAF life. After this they went for basic training, sometimes to bases in the oddest of places like universities, theatres or the hotels and promenades of seaside towns.

▶ A young pilot under instruction at flying school, 1940.

JOHN

I was called up in September 1939. One of the first jobs I did was guard duty at my local airfield. We didn't have any proper weapons so I was armed with a chair leg. In October I was billeted in St John's College, Cambridge. We did drill around the gravel paths of the College.

RAF life often came as a shock to young recruits straight from home. They suddenly found themselves with prickly new uniforms, early morning route marches, endless drill, lots of PE and yelling sergeants everywhere.

TOM

I had my first punishment when I overstayed my leave to see my sister. She was in the WAAF and was coming home just as I was due to return. I really wanted to see her, well, in case the worst happened and I didn't make it [was killed in action]. I was given three days jankers. I had to report every two hours with a full pack, clean the bedpans in hospital and peel potatoes in the kitchen.

RON

I was billeted in the Shakespeare Hotel in Stratford-upon-Avon. We did most of our drill on the forecourt of the famous Swan Theatre. We also had lessons in Morse Code, navigation and theory of flight.

▲ A forced landing on the sea was highly dangerous. This bomber crew is training how to use a rubber dinghy.

Flight Schools

After basic training, aircrew went on to flight schools. In 1939 the RAF was short of pilots, but other crewmen were vital too – navigators, bomb-aimers, radio operators and gunners. Britain is a difficult place to learn to fly – a small and cramped island with poor weather. Blinded by fog, rain and snow, many trainees died in accidents, smashing their planes into hills or runways.

RON

I had my first flying lessons at Wolverhampton airport and went solo after six hours. After this I was sent to Rhodesia. I got my pilot's licence after 80 hours flying a Cornell trainer. I was anxious in case I didn't make it, and every now and again a friend would be scrubbed from the course.

▶ Ron (sitting in the cockpit) and friends next to a Cornell trainer in Rhodesia, July 1944.

In 1940 the Empire Training Scheme was set up to make use of the wide-open spaces of Canada, Australia or southern Africa. Once abroad, aircrew had better weather and were safe from German attack.

▲ RAF air gunners training with a model on a pole and a camera gun. They would go on to serve in bomber crews.

Fighters

Fighters, like the Spitfire or twin-engined Whirlwind, were fast single-seater interceptor planes. Their job was to shoot down enemy bombers or their fighter plane escorts. The public image of fighter pilots was of devil-may-care heroes, but that was only part of the truth. The pilots fought a lonely war, crammed into a tight cockpit that might well become their coffin. In a dog-fight fast reactions and a level head were more important than taking risks. They had to be ruthless, hitting the enemy hard and without regret.

RON

I qualified as a fighter pilot after 200 hours training. This included gunnery practice – making ground attacks, dive-bombing with dummy bombs and mock dog-fights. The planes were fitted with cameras and if you got a clear photograph of your opponent from the right position, this showed you could have shot him down. Training like this was vital to keep you alive.

▶ A flight of Harvard trainers in Rhodesia from Ron's photo album.

HARRY

In 1941 I was posted to 263 Squadron flying twin-engined Whirlwinds. Our job was to defend Bristol from air raids. We also did a few convoy patrols in the Bristol Channel. When you were 'at readiness' [on duty and ready to take-off] you slept fully clothed in the crew hut next to the planes. We did this in flights of two, a bit like working shifts. In the summer we just wore our shirts with a life-jacket on top. When we climbed into our cockpits we sat on our parachutes and our mechanics clipped us to them. Our helmets had the radio microphone built in.

▶ The twin-engined Westland Whirlwind was one of the fastest fighters used by the RAF.

▼ Fighter pilots run to their planes after the order to SCRAMBLE is given.

During the summer of 1940 a few hundred brave fighter pilots beat the German air force, the Luftwaffe, in the Battle of Britain and saved the country from invasion.

Bombers

Bombers were sent out to destroy enemy industries, military targets and sometimes cities. Bomber crews had to fly and fight as a team. The size of the crew depended on the plane: a Wellington carried five men, while a Lancaster needed seven. Constantly faced with danger they became very close and relied on each other. Discipline was relaxed and everyone called each other by their first names or nicknames.

TOM

RAF bomber crews picked themselves. All the aircrew were mixed in together for final training, like a melting pot. They met one another at lectures or over a pint afterwards. The pilot would pick his navigator and then they would select the rest of their crew together. A bomber crew became like a family, all on first name terms.

▲ Tom and his crew, beside their Wellington Bomber in 1944. Tom and the other gunner were British and the rest were from New Zealand.

Crews had to fly 30 'sorties' or bombing missions, with only a 50-50 chance of surviving a tour of duty. Amongst the worst missions were attacks on German cities like Cologne or Berlin.

JOHN

In 1941 I was posted to Egypt, flying Wellington bombers. I never felt so vulnerable as when sitting on an enemy searchlight beam.

The desert was littered with emergency landing grounds. On one mission we had to put down with engine failure. An armourer was sent to remove and defuse our load of 500lb [225 kg] bombs but he didn't have the right tools. So the rest of the crew and I set about removing the detonators with pliers. It was only later that it occurred to us that we had been rather silly to try this.

▶ John and his crew in front of their Wellington bomber. This shot was taken on a captured Italian airbase in North Africa.

For much of the war bombing raids took place at night when it was safer. Streams of bombers, often several hundred strong, were sent out night after night. Even in the dark they made an easy target and enemy fighters and anti-aircraft guns took a terrible toll.

BETTY

I was the driver for Squadron Leader McCarthy for a while. One night his bomber didn't come back from a raid and I waited up till 4:00 am, sitting outside the control tower. It was the first time someone I knew well didn't come home – horrifying. But the aircrew just got on with it. 'Well,' they said, 'there's more space in the locker room now.'

Jack of All Trades

Alongside the fighters and bombers, other RAF aircraft did a host of war-winning jobs. Coastal Command aircraft patrolled the grey waters of the Atlantic hunting for German submarines, or U-boats; transport planes delivered men and supplies; reconnaissance aircraft took vital photographs of enemy installations; and the pilots of Met (Meteorology) Flight gathered data for weather forecasting, flying in the worst of conditions.

▲ A page from John Mills' logbook showing the U-boat kill. A/S patrol means anti-submarine patrol.

HARRY

In August 1941 I was posted to Met Flight, part of Bomber Command. The data we gathered was used to forecast the weather for raids over Europe. I used to fly up to the Norwegian Coast. We had to fly level for two minutes to gather readings on the instruments and we took readings every 1,000 feet [300 m], as high as we could go. In winter it was terribly cold. We wore woollen long johns with silk linings, a leather, fur-lined jacket, trousers and boots. We carried hot Bovril in thermos flasks because the milk in tea curdled at altitude.

JOHN

On the 18 July 1944 I was navigator in a Catalina [seaplane] patrolling near the Lofoten Islands [near Arctic Norway]. We hadn't been there long when a U-boat came into the area on the surface. We attacked it with two depth-charges, hoping the combined explosions would crack the hull. Unfortunately the U-boat fought back with four 20 mm cannon. Our plane was hit over 400 times at point blank range – we had to fly over the sub at just 50 feet [15 m] to drop more depth-charges. Two of our crew were wounded and an engine put out of action. It was a hairy time.

▲ A Catalina seaplane. The Catalina was John's favourite plane. With a range of over 3,200 km (2,000 miles) it could hunt U-boats deep into the Atlantic Ocean.

A World War – Stationed Overseas

During the Second World War the British Empire faced three enemies at once – Germany, Italy and Japan. To meet the threat the RAF had to fight ferocious battles from Malta in the Mediterranean to Burma in the Far East. Convoys of ships carried thousands of servicemen to far-flung bases in a war that spanned the globe. Our veterans were sometimes posted to exotic or exciting places – but they didn't always enjoy the experience.

JOHN

In 1940 I went to Egypt by sea, sailing from Liverpool, to Freetown in Sierra Leone then round the Cape of Good Hope. After this I was based at Abu Sueir and volunteered to deliver a Blenheim bomber to Port Sudan on the Red Sea Coast. Unfortunately I caught dysentery and had to go into hospital for two weeks to recover. The journey home was quite an epic. I had to wait a week to catch the train back to Waida Halfa and then a Nile steamer back to Aswan. There was a notice on the boat not to shoot crocodiles between 2:00 and 4:00pm – siesta time.

► John in uniform poses on a balcony in Athens.

▼ Tom was based in Gibraltar at the end of the war and visited Tangiers in nearby Morocco. He had this souvenir photo taken with a young Arab boy.

RON

In November 1944 it took us three weeks to get from a cold, wintry Scotland to Durban in South Africa where the temperature was 90 degrees in the shade. What a change! We travelled in a convoy through the Med to the Suez Canal and down to the Red Sea. We were attacked twice. It was very noisy with the pom-poms [anti-aircraft guns] going. The ship next to us was surrounded by plumes of water from near misses. I could see the coast of Africa on the horizon and reckoned that if my boat was hit I could swim for it.

▼ British servicemen boarding a ship to sail home from South Africa at the end of the war. Taken by Ron Watts.

Aircraft Down

The enemy were not the only problem for aircrew. All of our veterans flew in aircraft that broke down or crash-landed. Luckily they survived to tell their stories, but sadly others didn't. In Bomber Command alone, 8,000 aircrew were killed in training or accidents. With thousands of aircraft flying every day, this death rate was not surprising. Accidents were usually caused by mistakes made by pilots, bad weather or sheer bad luck.

TOM

One of the worst things I saw happened to an Ozzie [Australian] crew. They had almost finished a tour of duty and were coming in to land. The pilot overshot the runway and hit the NAAFI wagon. The plane crashed into a farm building and exploded. They were an experienced crew too.

▶ Lancaster Bomber 'T for Tilly' was shot up and crash-landed after a raid over Germany in 1943. Here the Repair and Maintenance Service are dismantling the plane.

HARRY

On 14 May 1942 I was flying back from Norway below 200 feet [62 m] because of poor visibility. There aren't many hills in Norfolk but there was one between base and us. The air intake blocked with ice and one engine cut out. I couldn't gain height on the remaining engine to get over the hill, so I picked a nice field to land in. But there was a telephone wire in the way! I got the nose of the Blenheim over but the tail wheel caught and we cartwheeled. The navigator went out through the nose and broke his leg. I put my head through the cockpit roof and needed 38 stitches.

▲ The wreckage of Harry's plane. Amazingly all the crew survived.

Keeping Us Flying

RAF aircrew were only the steel tip of an enormous war effort. Planes had to be maintained and repaired, air bases to be built and protected, raids to be planned. In addition, crews had to be fed and kept supplied with water and other necessities in often inhospitable terrain. An average base for two squadrons of bombers had about 1,000 ground crew. Our veterans have nothing but praise for those who worked hard on the ground to keep them flying.

▲ These WAAFs were qualified pilots. They were not allowed to fight but were used to ferry aircraft to RAF stations.

HARRY

RAF food was good as long as you liked what you were given. In Norfolk we were fed eel but I couldn't stomach that. On operations we had bacon and eggs. Eggs were rare so that was a real perk for the crews.

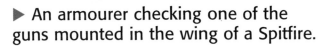
▶ An armourer checking one of the guns mounted in the wing of a Spitfire.

The role of the Women's Auxiliary Air Force (WAAF) was vital. WAAFs never flew in combat missions, but by the end of the war they were involved in key support jobs such as weather forecasting, reading enemy codes, manning operations rooms, driving and delivering planes to airfields.

BETTY

I drove a Fordson lorry for A flight, 466 Squadron. I was the 'go for' – I had to pick up the ground staff to service and repair the planes, sometimes at 5:30 in the morning. Then I picked up spare parts, took anyone injured to sick bay, ran the fellas back for meals – that sort of thing.

◀ Betty and the RAF squadron she served with.

▼ John sleeping in a tent in the North African desert. To make standing height in the tents, the ground was dug out for 60cm (two feet) underneath them.

JOHN

In the desert, water had to be transported out to us by lorry. We had one pint [0.5l] a day to wash, shave and wash our clothes. You'd be having a shave and someone would yell, 'Don't throw that water away, I've got a pair of socks to wash.'

Feet on the Ground

The RAF realized aircrew needed regular breaks. Flying and fighting were stressful and it was important for them to relax. Leisure activities varied depending on where they were stationed. In England, crews might be on a bombing raid over Germany one night and in the pub having a pint the next.

TOM

I had my first leave in June 1944. I had my sergeant's tapes on and felt very proud. I was asked out for a drink and had three pints. I was quite merry but was afraid to go home. Even though I was an adult and in the RAF I knew my mother would disapprove. I walked around till I sobered up.

Letters from wives or sweethearts, films and concerts or a game of football were all good for morale, but best of all was leave. This might be a short break in a local town or, for the lucky ones, a visit home.

◀ John and his new bride Margaret in 1942. Couples often only had a few days to arrange their wedding during wartime.

JOHN

When I was stationed in North Africa we used to go on leave in Palestine, to Tel Aviv [now in Israel]. Just before Christmas 1941 we flew there in a Wellington and loaded up with oranges. We flew back with enough for the whole camp.

▶ John and friends sunbathing in Palestine.

▼ RAF servicemen pulling crackers at a Christmas Party in 1942.

RON

My parents wrote regularly and I sent them food parcels from Rhodesia, treats like tinned fruit. Music was very important in lonely places. I was musical and played the piano in the mess virtually very night – popular hits like *White Cliffs of Dover* or *Thanks for that Lovely Weekend*. I got to know everybody because of my playing.

Memories to Last a Lifetime

Our veterans saw many grim sights, like ruined cities or friends who had been killed. Even so, their memories more often turn to proud or happy events. They were young and life was rich in experience.

As Ron commented: 'We all joined up as lads and came back as men. We were given an opportunity to stretch ourselves that we would never have had in civilian life.'

HARRY

A good memory was finding a Wellington that had ditched in the sea when we were coming back from a flight to Norway. We circled to look for the crew and sent a radio signal. Our navigator gave a good fix for air-sea rescue and they were saved.

▼ Harry sitting on the wing of a Hudson bomber in September 1942.

RON

The climate in Rhodesia was perfect. No one said, 'Nice day' – it was always a nice day! You could plan a picnic three months in advance and know it wouldn't have to be called off. The average housewife in London had a harder war.

TOM

I met Ruby, the lady who became my wife, when I was home on leave for Christmas. The RAF uniform was good for attracting girls. A bunch of us went to a dance a few miles away and missed the last bus home. We got to know one another on the long walk back. I was never a good dancer, but I was a good taker-homer.

▶ A Walrus amphibian aeroplane is loaded with blankets and warm clothing by an air-sea rescue squadron in preparation for a rescue trip.

JOHN MILLS

When we were hunting submarines in the Catalina, the flights could be very long – 15 hour patrols in winter, often flying at just 500 feet [150 m]. We had a metal box with two camping stoves in it and someone would cook up a fried breakfast – wonderful.

De-mob and a Post-war World

Germany surrendered in May 1945 and Japan in August. Within months, millions of British servicemen and women were de-mobbed and trying to fit back into civilian life. It wasn't always easy. After the excitement of wartime flying, family life and work often seemed dull.

JOHN

After the war I worked for a British airline, BOAC, as a navigator and trainer. In 1965 I got a job with Lufthansa, a German airline. That made me smile. I still go to Aircrew Association reunions and enjoy talking about service days.

▼ First and Second World War planes are top attractions at aircraft museums like Shuttleworth.

BETTY

If I hadn't got married I would have stayed on in the WAAF. I loved the RAF. Settling down to my old job and family life was difficult. It might seem odd to say it, but for me the war had been a great adventure.

▼ John Mills' war medals, including the Africa Star, which was awarded to servicemen who fought in the desert war against the Italians and Germans.

Our veterans all agree that they fought a just war against an evil enemy and, in spite of the danger, had a good time. But they are the survivors. When they meet up with old comrades they always spare a thought for the friends who didn't make it.

HARRY

I was de-mobbed in February 1946 and went back to work in insurance, but found it very hard to settle down to civilian life. I've hardly flown in a plane since the war, even on holidays. I don't like being a passenger with another pilot.

Glossary

Armourer weapons mechanic.

Battle of the Atlantic the war against German submarines in the Atlantic Ocean.

Bedpans toilets for patients who are not well enough to get out of bed.

Called up ordered to join the armed forces.

Conscription being ordered to join the armed services by the government.

Convoy ships travelling together in groups so they could be protected from air or submarine attacks.

Defuse make harmless by removing the detonators that triggered the bombs.

De-mob leave the armed services.

Depth-charge a bomb that could be set to explode under the sea.

Drill marching and other exercises.

Empire parts of the world ruled by Britain, like India or Malaya.

Intercept catch and destroy.

Jankers slang for punishment.

Leave time off for home visits.

Long johns warm underwear, similar to pyjamas.

Luftwaffe German air force.

Mess club house.

Morale fighting spirit, the mental strength to continue fighting.

Morse Code a system using long and short signals to spell out letters.

NAAFI catering service run by the Navy, Army and Air Force Institute.

Navigator the crewman who kept the plane on the right route during a journey.

Reconnaissance taking a close look at enemy territory.

Recruits new members of the air force, ready to be trained.

Scramble take-off at once.

Tour of duty time spent in dangerous operations.

U-boats German submarines.

Veterans retired members of the armed services.

Volunteer reserve a part-time member of the RAF, ready to be called up if there was a war.

Wings a badge indicating that someone is a fully trained RAF pilot.

Further Reading

Non-fiction

Beck, Pip, *A WAAF in Bomber Command*, Goodall Publications, 1989.

Harvey, Anne, *In Time of War*, MacMillan, 2000.

Hepplewhite, Peter, *A World in Flames: World War II in the Air*, MacMillan, 2001.

Nesbit, Roy Conyers, *An Illustrated History of the RAF*, Salamander Books, 2002.

Fiction

Eldridge, J., *Deadly Skies*, Puffin, 1999.

Swindells, Robert, *Hurricane Summer*, Mammoth, 1997.

Westall, Robert, *The Machine Gunners*, Macmillan, 1999.

Resources

Places to Visit

The Imperial War Museum Duxford, Cambridge.

The RAF Museum, Grahame Park Road, Hendon.

The RAF Museum, Cosford, Shifnal, Shropshire.

390th Bomb Group Memorial Air Museum, Parham Airfield, Parham, Woodbridge, Suffolk.

The Shuttleworth Collection, Old Warden Park, Biggleswade, Bedfordshire.

Index

Numbers in *italics* indicate photographs.